BASICALL BLUE

a collection of blueberry recipes

FERN WALKER

Published by Creative Bound Inc.

Box 424, Carp, Ontario, Canada K0A 1L0
(613) 831-3641
1-800-287-8610 (toll free)
Email: orderdesk@creativebound.com
www.creativebound.com

ISBN 0-921165-00-5
Printed and bound in Canada

First Printing April 1986
Twelfth Printing, July 2007

Designed by Wendy O'Keefe
copyright © by Fern Walker

No part of this book may be reproduced, stored in a retrieval system
or transmitted in any form by any means electronic, mechanical,
photocopying, recording or otherwise, except for purposes of review,
without the prior permission of the publisher.

Canadian Cataloguing in Publication Data

Walker, Fern, 1938-

Basically Blue

Includes index
ISBN 0-921165-00-5

1. Cookery (Blueberries). I. Title

TX813.BW34 1986   641.6'4737   C86-090167-X

A Letter of Introduction from
Nova Scotia's Minister of
Agriculture & Marketing

Wild blueberries have been a part of Fern Walker's life ever since she can remember. She was born in Millvale, Nova Scotia, right in the centre of that province's largest blueberry producing region. Her father, Carvell Stonehouse, was involved in Nova Scotia's blueberry industry for fifty-one years as a grower, buyer and industry leader. He used to proudly tell the story that Fern first became involved while still in her highchair. She would help put the cellophane covers on the quarts of fresh wild blueberries that her father was shipping to central Canadian markets.

In the years since then, Fern has worked at "every job in the business", from harvesting the fruit in the fields to her present job of promoting wild blueberries in Ontario for the Blueberry Producers' Association of Nova Scotia.

Fern and her husband, Paul, have four children. The family has lived in Ottawa for the past eighteen years, but they still think of themselves as Maritimers.

We in Nova Scotia are very proud of our wild blueberries. This unique fruit is becoming increasingly popular all over the world. We are also extremely proud to have Fern Walker as our "wild blueberry ambassador in Ottawa". In Fern's own words: "When you have a good product that you are proud of you want to share it with everyone."

It is my pleasure as Minister of Agriculture and Marketing for the province of Nova Scotia to recommend this book containing Fern's own collection of delicious recipes using Nova Scotia wild blueberries.

Sincerely,

Hon. Roger Bacon,
Minister of Agriculture
and Marketing
Province of Nova Scotia

Thanks to everyone who assisted in the production of this book —
Many thanks to all my friends and relatives who shared their favourite recipes.
Thanks to OXFORD FROZEN FOODS for supplying all the berries I used in testing.
A special thanks to my family for their co-operation especially for testing the "hits" and the "misses"!

This book is dedicated to the memory of my father, Carvell Stonehouse a man who shared so much with many people.

Table of Contents

Muffins 1

Breads~Biscuits 13

Desserts 23

Cookies ~ Squares 55

Etcetera 61

Muffins

BLUEBERRY BUTTERMILK MUFFINS

3/4 cup	all-purpose flour	175 mL
3/4 cup	whole wheat flour	175 mL
1 1/4 cups plus		300 mL plus
1 1/2 tsp.	white sugar	7 mL
1/4 cup	oil	50 mL
1/2 cup	buttermilk	125 mL
1 cup	blueberries	250 mL
1/2 tsp.	baking powder	2 mL
1/2 tsp.	baking soda	2 mL
1/2 tsp.	salt	2 mL
1	egg, beaten	1
1/2 cup	honey	125 mL
1 tsp.	vanilla	5 mL

Preheat oven to 350°F (180°C).
Mix dry ingredients together.
Add liquids and stir until just moistened.
Fold in blueberries.
Bake for 15 minutes.
Remove from oven, sprinkle tops with pinch of sugar.
Return to oven and bake for 15 to 20 minutes longer.

Makes 12 to 18 medium muffins.

BLUEBERRY PUMPKIN MUFFINS

3 cups	all-purpose flour	750 mL
1 cup	white sugar	250 mL
1 tbsp.	cinnamon	15 mL
2 tsp.	baking powder	10 mL
2 tsp.	baking soda	10 mL
1 tsp.	salt	5 mL
3	eggs, slightly beaten	3
1 cup	oil	250 mL
1 3/4 cups	pumpkin	425 mL
2 cups	blueberries	500 mL

Preheat oven to 375°F (190°C).

Grease muffin tins, dust with flour.

Mix dry ingredients in a large bowl.

Mix eggs, oil and pumpkin together and add liquid ingredients to dry ingredients.

Add blueberries and stir until batter is combined.

Bake for 15-20 minutes and sprinkle tops with brown sugar if desired.

Makes 30 to 36 medium muffins.

NOTE: For microwave cooking, bake on High for 4 minutes, rotating pan halfway through cooking time.

BLUEBERRY OATMEAL MUFFINS

1 1/4 cups	quick oats	300 mL
1 cup	all-purpose flour	250 mL
1/3 cup	white sugar	75 mL
1 tbsp.	baking powder	15 mL
1/2 tsp.	salt	2 mL
1 cup	milk	250 mL
1	egg	1
1/4 cup	oil	50 mL
1 cup	blueberries	250 mL

Preheat oven to 425°F (220°C).
Grease muffin tins, dust with flour.
Combine dry ingredients in large bowl.
Mix milk, egg and oil, add to dry ingredients.
Fold in blueberries.
Bake for 25 minutes.

Makes 18 to 24 muffins.

NOTE: If using frozen blueberries, put them in directly from freezer, not allowing to thaw.

One cup of wild blueberries supplies nearly 1/3 of an adult's daily requirement of Vitamin C.

SHARON'S BLUEBERRY MUFFINS

3 cups	all-purpose flour	750 mL
1 cup	white sugar	250 mL
2 1/2 tsp.	baking powder	12 mL
1/2 tsp.	salt	2 mL
2 or 3	large eggs	2 or 3
1 1/2 cups	milk	375 mL
2/3 cup	butter, melted	150 mL
2 cups	blueberries	500 mL
1 tbsp.	lemon rind, grated	15 mL
2 tbsp.	white sugar	30 mL

Preheat oven to 400°F (200°C).
Grease 18 large or 24 medium muffin tins, dust with flour.
Mix together flour, baking powder, salt and sugar in a large bowl.
In a small bowl, beat eggs, add milk and melted butter.
Add liquid ingredients to dry ingredients and stir until just moistened.
Stir in blueberries.
Spoon into muffin tins, filling them 3/4 full.
Combine lemon rind with sugar and sprinkle over top.
Bake for 20 minutes or until the tops of muffins spring back when touched.

BLUEBERRY BRAN MUFFINS

2 cups	all-purpose flour	500 mL
2 cups	bran	500 mL
1 cup	white sugar	250 mL
2 tbsp.	molasses	30 mL
1 tsp.	baking soda	5 mL
1 cup	blueberries	250 mL
1	egg, well beaten	1
1 tsp.	salt	5 mL
2 tbsp.	shortening	30 mL
1 1/2 cups	sour milk	375 mL

(sweet milk may be used if 1 tbsp. (15 mL) of baking powder is used instead of the soda).

Preheat oven to 375°F (190°C).
Mix shortening with molasses and sugar.
Add egg, milk, salt, flour, bran, soda and blueberries.
Bake in well-greased muffin tins for 10 to 15 minutes.

Makes up to 36 muffins.

MICROWAVE BLUEBERRY MUFFINS

2 cups	all-purpose flour	500 mL
1/4 cup	white sugar	50 mL
2 tsp.	baking powder	10 mL
1/4 tsp.	baking soda	1 mL
1/2 tsp.	salt	2 mL
3/4 cup	orange juice	175 mL
1/4 cup	oil	50 mL
1	egg	1
1 tsp.	orange rind, grated	5 mL
2 cups	blueberries	500 mL

Combine dry indredients; mix remaining ones in a separate bowl.
Add the liquid mixture to the dry ingredients and stir until slightly moistened.

Microwave, uncovered, for 3 to 4 minutes, rotating dish after 1 ½ to 2 minutes, if baking unevenly.

If desired, sprinkle the following nut topping over muffins before cooking: **1/4 cup (50 mL) brown sugar, 1/3 cup (75 mL) chopped pecans, and 1/2 tsp. (2 mL) cinnamon.**

Makes 18 to 24 medium muffins.

JIFFY BLUEBERRY MUFFINS

1 1/2 cups	all-purpose flour	375 mL
1 1/2 tsp.	cinnamon	7 mL
1 tsp.	baking powder	5 mL
1 tsp.	baking soda	5 mL
1/2 tsp.	salt	2 mL
1/2 cup	white sugar	125 mL
1 cup	blueberry sauce (see page 63)	250 mL
2	eggs	2
3/4 cup	oil	175 mL
	grated orange or lemon rind	

Preheat oven to 400°F (200°C).
Mix all ingredients together until just moistened.
Bake for 20 minutes.

Makes 12 to 18 medium muffins.

Puree frozen berries in a blender. Pour into square pan and store in refrigerator. Use as flavouring in sauces, icings, fruit toppings, etc.

BLUEBERRY MAPLE MUFFINS WITH STREUSEL TOPPING

1 1/2 cups	all-purpose flour	375 mL
1/4 cup	white sugar	50 mL
1 tbsp.	baking powder	15 mL
1/2 tsp.	salt	2 mL
1/4 cup	butter, melted	50 mL
1	egg, beaten	1
1/2 cup	milk	125 mL
1/2 cup	maple syrup	125 mL
3/4 cup	quick oats	175 mL
1 cup	blueberries	250 mL

Preheat oven to 400°F (200°C).
Sift together flour, sugar, baking powder and salt.
Blend butter, beaten egg, milk, syrup and oats.
Stir in dry mixture until all ingredients are just moistened.
Fold in blueberries.
Fill well-greased or lined muffin tins 2/3 full with batter.
Dot with Streusel Topping.
Bake for 35 to 40 minutes.

Makes 12 muffins.

Streusel Topping

2 tbsp.	butter	30 mL
2 tbsp.	brown sugar	30 mL
1 tsp.	cinnamon	5 mL
1/4 cup	nuts, finely chopped	50 mL

Melt butter in small saucepan.
Stir in sugar, cinnamon and nuts.
Blend well.

ANNA'S BLUEBERRY MUFFINS

1 1/2 cups	all-purpose flour	375 mL
1/2 cup	white sugar	125 mL
1/4 cup	butter, softened	50 mL
2 tsp.	baking powder	10 mL
1/2 tsp.	salt	2 mL
1	egg	1
1/2 cup	milk	125 mL
1 1/2 cup	blueberries	375 mL

Preheat oven to 400°F (200°C).
Cream together butter and sugar.
Add egg.
Mix dry ingredients together and fold into butter mixture alternately with milk.
Fold in blueberries.

Top with the following mixture:

> **2 tbsp. (30 mL) butter, melted**
> **2 tbsp. (30 mL) brown sugar**
> **1/4 tsp. (1 mL) cinnamon**
> **1/4 cup (50 mL) nuts, finely chopped**

Bake for 20 to 25 minutes.
Makes a dozen medium-size muffins.

Breads ~ Biscuits

BLUEBERRY BISCUITS

2 cups	all-purpose flour	500 mL
3/4 tsp.	salt	4 mL
3 tsp.	baking powder	15 mL
1/2 cup	shortening	125 mL
2/3 cup	milk	150 mL
1/4 cup	blueberries	50 mL

Preheat oven to 425°F (220°C).
Combine dry ingredients and work in shortening.
Add enough milk to just mix.
Cut dough into rounds. Press a few berries into dough.
Bake for 15-20 minutes.

BLUEBERRY SCOTCH SCONES

3 cups	all-purpose flour	750 mL
2 tsp.	baking powder	10 mL
3/4 cup	white sugar	175 mL
1/4 tsp.	salt	1 mL
3/4 cup	butter, softened	175 mL
1	egg, well beaten, combined with enough milk to make 1 cup (250 mL)	1
1 cup	blueberries	250 mL

Preheat oven to 450°F (230°C).
Combine flour, salt, and baking powder.
Cream butter and add sugar gradually.
Add dry ingredients and egg mixture alternately to butter mixture.
Fold blueberries into batter.
Roll out to 1/4" and cut into biscuits.
Bake for 12 minutes.

Pears (sliced or cubed) added to blueberries in pies are very good.

MARJORIE'S BLUEBERRY ORANGE BREAD

2 tbsp.	butter	30 mL
1/4 cup	boiling water	50 mL
1/2 cup	orange juice	125 mL
1 tbsp.	orange rind, grated	15 mL
1	egg	1
1 cup	white sugar	250 mL
2 cups	all-purpose flour	500 mL
1 tsp.	baking powder	5 mL
1/4 tsp.	baking soda	1 mL
1/2 tsp.	salt	2 mL
1 cup	blueberries	250 mL

Sauce:

2 tbsp.	orange juice	30 mL
1 tsp.	orange rind, grated	5 mL
2 tbsp.	honey	30 mL

Preheat oven to 325°F (160°C).
Add butter to boiling water and stir until melted.
Stir in orange juice and orange rind.
Beat egg with sugar.
Add dry ingredients to egg mixture alternately with orange liquid.
Fold in blueberries.
Bake for 1 hour and 10 minutes.
Remove from pan when baked.
Combine sauce ingredients and spoon over loaf.

BLUEBERRY GINGERBREAD

1/2 cup	**butter, softened**	125 mL
1/2 cup	**brown sugar**	125 mL
2	**eggs, beaten**	2
2 cups	**all-purpose flour**	500 mL
1 tbsp.	**baking powder**	15 mL
1/4 tsp.	**salt**	2 mL
2 tsp.	**ginger**	10 mL
1 tsp.	**cinnamon**	5 mL
1/2 cup	**sour cream**	125 mL
1/2 cup	**molasses**	125 mL
1 1/2 cups	**blueberries**	375 mL

Preheat oven to 350°F (180°C).

Grease an 8'' (20 cm) square baking pan and dust with flour.

Cream butter, add sugar and eggs gradually and mix well.

Sift together dry ingredients and add alternately with combined sour cream and molasses to the creamed mixture.

Fold in blueberries.

Put batter in pan.

Bake 45 minutes, remove from oven and brush with melted butter.

Variation:

Make gingerbread cupcakes by spooning batter into lined muffin tins. Bake at 350°F (180°C) for approximately 20 minutes, or until cooked. Makes 12 cupcakes.

JOYCE'S BLUEBERRY TEA LOAVES

6	eggs	6
4 cups	white sugar	1 L
1 1/2 cups	milk	375 mL
1 1/2 tbsp.	cinnamon	20 mL
10 tsp.	baking powder	50 mL
1 tsp.	salt	5 mL
8 cups	all-purpose flour	2 L
4 cups	blueberries	1 L

Preheat oven to 350°F (180°C).
In a large bowl, beat eggs and gradually add sugar.
Stir in milk and blend in dry ingredients.
Fold in floured blueberries.
Spoon batter into 4 greased and floured loaf pans.
Bake for 50 to 60 minutes or until centre fells firm to touch.
If desired, decorate loaves with one of the following toppings.

Frosting:

1 cup	icing sugar	250 mL
	milk, just enough to thicken	
1 tsp.	cinnamon	5 mL

Mix icing sugar with milk just to thicken.
Stir in cinnamon and spread on loaves. Dry at room temperature.

Sugar topping:

1/3 cup	white sugar	75 mL
2 tbsp.	lemon juice	30 mL

. . . continued next page

JOYCE'S BLUEBERRY TEA LOAVES

Continued . . .

Mix sugar and lemon juice.
Spoon mixture over loaf tops, allowing time for mixture to absorb.

Coconut:

1/4 cup	icing sugar	50 mL
	orange juice to thicken	
	grated rind of 1 orange	
1/3 cup	coconut	75 mL

Mix icing sugar with orange juice just to thicken.
Stir in orange rind.
Spread mixture on loaves and sprinkle with coconut.

ANNE'S ORANGE BLUE LOAF

1 1/2 cups	white sugar	375 mL
1/2 cup	butter, softened	125 mL
2	eggs	2
1 1/2 tsp.	baking powder	7 mL
1/2 tsp.	salt	2 mL
2 cups	all-purpose flour	500 mL
1/2 cup	orange juice	125 mL
	grated rind of 1 orange	
3/4 cup	blueberries	175 mL

Preheat oven to 350°F (180°C).
Cream butter and add sugar gradually.
Beat in eggs. Stir in orange juice and rind.
In another bowl, combine dry ingredients.
Add to orange juice mixture.
Fold in blueberries.
Bake for 1 hour.

LEMON BLUEBERRY LOAF

1 cup	white sugar	250 mL
1/2 cup	butter, softened	125 mL
2	eggs	2
1 1/2 cups	all-purpose flour	375 mL
1/4 tsp.	salt	1 mL
1 tsp.	baking powder	5 mL
	grated rind of 1 lemon	
1/2 cup	milk	125 mL
1 cup	blueberries	250 mL

Topping:

1/4 cup	white sugar	50 mL
	juice from 1 lemon	

Preheat oven to 350°F (180°C).
Cream butter and stir in sugar a bit at a time.
Beat in eggs.
In a bowl, combine dry ingredients and lemon rind.
Add this mixture alternately with milk to the butter mixture.
Fold in blueberries.
Bake 1 hour.
Remove from pan and spoon topping on hot loaf.

Desserts

HOPE'S NO BAKE BLUEBERRY PIE

2 cups	**blueberries**	**500 mL**
19 oz. tin	**blueberry pie filling or blueberry sauce (see page 63)**	**540 mL**
One 9''	**baked pie shell or graham wafer crust**	**One 20 cm (approximately)**
1 cup	**whipped cream or dessert topping**	**250 mL**

Fold blueberries into pie filling or sauce.
Pour mixture into baked pie shell.
Top with whipped cream or dessert topping.

Serves six to eight.

Blueberries are Nature's most perfect fruit — no peeling, no pits, no cores — an easy day for the cook!

BLUEBERRY PIE

Shortbread base:

1 cup	**all-purpose flour**	**250 mL**
2 tbsp.	**icing sugar**	**30 mL**
1/2 cup	**butter**	**125 mL**

Preheat oven to 425°F (220°C).
Sift flour and icing sugar together and cut in butter.
Chill dough for 30 minutes and press firmly into pie plate.
Bake for 10 to 12 minutes.
Cool base before filling.

Filling:

5 tbsp.	**all-purpose flour**	**75 mL**
pinch	**salt**	**pinch**
1/4 cup	**water**	**50 mL**
1 cup	**blueberries**	**250 mL**
3/4 cup	**white sugar**	**175 mL**
1/2 cup	**water**	**125 mL**
3 cups	**blueberries**	**750 mL**
	whipped cream (optional)	
	grated lemon rind (optional)	

Make paste of flour, salt and 1/4 cup (50 mL) water.
Stir paste into 1 cup (250 mL) berries, add sugar and 1/2 cup (125 mL) water, bring to a boil; lower heat to medium and cook until it thickens, stirring constantly.
Remove from heat and stir in 3 cups (750 mL) blueberries.
Pour mixture into pie shell.
Cool.
If desired, top with whipped cream mixed with a little grated lemon rind.

STONEHOUSE BLUEBERRY PIE

4 cups	blueberries	1 L
2/3 cup	white sugar	150 mL
1 tbsp.	minute tapioca	15 mL
2 tbsp.	pastry flour	30 mL
pinch	salt	pinch
dot	butter	dot
sprinkle	lemon juice	sprinkle
1	unbaked pie shell	1

Preheat oven to 450°F (230°C).

Mix together above ingredients and pour into an unbaked pie shell.

Bake at 450°F (230°C) for 10 minutes, then reduce heat to 350°F (180°C) and bake for another 30 minutes.

ORANGE'N BERRY SPONGE PIE

2/3 cup	white sugar	150 mL
2 tbsp.	all-purpose flour	30 mL
1 tbsp.	butter	15 mL
	juice and rind of 1 orange	

Mix the above four ingredients together.

2	eggs, separated	2
3/4 cup	milk	175 mL
1 cup	blueberries	250 mL
1	unbaked pie shell	1

Preheat oven to 350°F (180°C).
Beat egg yolks and milk together and add to orange mixture.
Beat egg whites until they form stiff peaks; fold into batter.
Fold in blueberries.
Place mixture in unbaked pie shell.
Bake for 40-50 minutes.

MAC'S FAVOURITE BLUEBERRY CREAM PIE

Shell:

1 1/2 cups	graham wafer crumbs	375 mL
1/2 cup	butter	125 mL

Preheat oven to 350°F (180°C).
Mix ingredients together and press into pie plate.
Bake for 10 minutes.
Cool.

Filling:

40	miniature marshmallows	40
2 cups	blueberries	500 mL
3/4 cup	milk	175 mL
1 cup	dessert topping, whipped	250 mL
	grated lemon or orange rind	

Melt marshmallows and milk over hot water.
Add rind.
Cool thoroughly.
Add blueberries.
Fold in topping.
Pour over baked crumb mixture.
Sprinkle graham wafer crumbs on top.

JEAN'S POUND CAKE

1 3/4 cups	white sugar	425 mL
1 cup	butter, softened	250 mL
3	eggs	3
2 tsp.	almond flavouring	10 mL
3 1/2 cups	all-purpose flour, sifted	875 mL
1/2 tsp.	salt	2 mL
1 1/2 tsp.	baking powder	7 mL
1 cup	warm milk	250 mL

Preheat oven to 325°F (160°C).
Cream butter and sugar.
Add eggs, one at a time.
Add dry ingredients alternately with warm milk.
Add flavouring.
Bake in 2 loaf pans for approximately 1 hour.

BLUEBERRY SAUCE
(for trifle)

1/2 cup	white sugar	125 mL
pinch	salt	pinch
2 to 3 tsp.	cornstarch	10 to 15 mL
1/2 cup	water	125 mL
3 cups	blueberries	750 mL

Stir together sugar, salt and cornstarch.

With a whisk, stir in water and cook over medium high heat.

When ingredients are dissolved, add blueberries and stir constantly until mixture comes to a boil.

Simmer and stir until thickened and clear (approximately 4 minutes).

Cool, covered with lid or plastic wrap.

One hundred grams of blueberries contain only 51 calories, and no colesterol!

GRAM'S CORNSTARCH PUDDING

2	**eggs, beaten**	2
1/4 **cup**	**white sugar**	50 mL
2 cups	**milk**	500 mL
2 tbsp.	**cornstarch**	30 mL
1 tsp.	**vanilla**	5 mL
pinch	**salt**	pinch

Beat eggs in top of double boiler.
Add sugar, cornstarch and salt.
Gradually stir in milk.
Cook over hot (not boiling) water until mixture begins to thicken.
Add vanilla and set in refrigerator to cool.

Be daring — add frozen wild blueberries to your favourite recipes!

WALKER'S SPECIAL TRIFLE

1 recipe	**Gram's Cornstarch Pudding** (see page 30) or 1 package (lg.) vanilla pudding and pie mix	1 recipe
1/2 **recipe**	pound cake (see page 28)	1/2 **recipe**
4 tbsp.	pear brandy liqueur	60 mL
1 recipe	blueberry sauce (see page 63)	250 mL
1 cup	heavy cream	250 mL

Prepare pudding and set in refrigerator to cool covered with plastic wrap.

Bake pound cakes (one to use for trifle).

Cook blueberry sauce.

Assemble:

Cover bottom of glass bowl with thin layers of pound cake.

Spoon blueberry sauce over cake (just enough to cover).

Sprinkle 1 1/2 tbsp. (20 mL) liqueur over berries.

Spread enough pudding in dish to cover berries.

Repeat this layering until dish is full.

Refrigerate until chilled.

Whip cream, adding 1 tsp. (5 mL) of vanilla or liqueur for flavouring.

Heap cream on top of trifle.

Serves ten or more.

MARK'S CHEESECAKE

1 3/4 cups	graham wafer crumbs	425 mL
1/2 cup	butter, melted	125 mL
1/2 tsp.	cinnamon	2 mL
1/4 cup	nuts, chopped	50 mL

Combine ingredients and press into bottom of a spring-form pan.

Topping:

3	eggs	3
8 oz. pkg.	cream cheese, softened	250 g.
2/3 cup	white sugar	150 mL
1 tsp.	vanilla	5 mL
2 cups	sour cream	500 mL
1 pkg.	glaze mix	1 pkg.
2 cups	blueberries	500 mL

Preheat oven to 375°F (190°C).
Beat first five ingredients together and pour over crust.
Bake for 50-60 minutes.
Cool.
Cover top with blueberries.
Prepare glaze according to package instructions and pour over blueberries.

PROMOTION CHEESECAKE

2 cups	graham wafer crumbs	500 mL
1/2 tsp.	cinnamon	2 mL
1/3 cup	pecans, chopped	75 mL
2/3 cup	butter, melted	150 mL
1	egg	1

Mix together and press into a large spring-form pan.

Topping:

4	eggs	4
2/3 cup	white sugar	150 mL
8 oz. pkg.	cream cheese, softened	250 g
1 1/2 tsp.	vanilla	7 mL
1 cup	plain yogurt	250 g
2 cups	sour cream	500 mL

Preheat oven to 375°F (190°C).
Beat all ingredients together and spread over base.
Bake for 1 hour.
Chill.
Cover with 3 cups (750 mL) blueberry sauce (see page 63).
When ready to serve, unmould onto serving plate and, if desired, top with whipped cream.

LINA'S CUPCAKE CHEESE CAKES

2 8 oz. pkgs.	**cream cheese, softened**	**2 250g. pkgs.**
3/4 cup	**white sugar**	**175 mL**
pinch	**salt**	**pinch**
3	**eggs**	**3**
1/2 tsp.	**vanilla**	**2 mL**
1 box	**vanilla wafers**	**1 box**
3 cups	**blueberries**	**750 mL**

Preheat oven to 350°F (180°C).
Cream together first five ingredients.
Put one wafer in bottom of each cupcake container.
Fill 3/4 full with mixture.
Bake 20 minutes.
Cool, then spread blueberries on top and seal with a glaze or cover cooled cakes with blueberry sauce (see page 63).

BLUEBERRY DESSERT

2 cups	all-purpose flour	500 mL
3/4 cup	white sugar	175 mL
1/2 tsp.	salt	2 mL
1 tbsp.	baking powder	15 mL
1/3 cup	shortening	75 mL
2 cups	blueberries	500 mL
2	eggs, well beaten	2
1 cup	milk	250 mL

Preheat oven to 350°F (180°C).

Sift together dry ingredients and cut in shortening with a pastry blender.

Mix eggs and milk and stir into flour mixture, blending into a dough.

Toss in blueberries with fork.

Put half the batter in square cake pan, top with berries, cover with remaining batter.

Bake for 25-35 minutes.

Serve with whipped cream or brown sugar sauce (see page 36).

BROWN SUGAR SAUCE

3/4 cup	brown sugar	175 mL
1 1/2 tbsp.	all-purpose flour	25 mL
pinch	salt	pinch
1 1/2 cups	boiling water	375 mL
1 1/2 tbsp.	butter	25 mL
1 1/2 tsp.	vanilla	7 mL
	dash of nutmeg (optional)	

Mix together sugar, flour and salt in saucepan.

Slowly add boiling water and stir over medium heat until thickened.

Simmer for 5 minutes, remove from heat, and stir in butter, vanilla and nutmeg (if desired).

EXHIBITION FAVOURITE YOGURT CAKE

1 cup	blueberry yogurt	250 g
1 cup	blueberries	250 mL
2 cups	all-purpose flour	500 mL
1/2 tsp.	baking powder	2 mL
1 tsp.	baking soda	5 mL
1 cup	brown sugar	250 mL
1/2 cup	butter, softened	125 mL
1	egg	1
3/4 tsp.	vanilla	4 mL

Preheat oven to 350°F (180°C).
In a large bowl, combine yogurt and blueberries and let stand.
Sift together flour, baking powder and baking soda.
Cream together sugar and butter.
Add 1 egg beaten with vanilla to sugar mixture.
Alternately combine dry and wet ingredients into yogurt mixture.
Bake for 45 minutes in a 9" x 13" pan.
Dust with a sprinkling of icing sugar.

Wild blueberries provide a taste all their own!

GWEN'S HURRY-UP CAKE

1/2 cup	milk, gently heated	125 mL
2 tbsp.	butter	30 mL
1/2 tsp.	vanilla	2 mL
2	eggs, well beaten	2
1 cup	white sugar	250 mL
1 1/4 cups	all-purpose flour	300 mL
1 tsp.	baking powder	5 mL
1/2 cup	blueberries	125 mL

Preheat oven to 350°F (180°C).
Sift together sugar, flour and baking powder.
Add butter and vanilla to heated milk.
Add dry ingredients to eggs, alternating with milk mixture.
Add blueberries.
Bake for 35 minutes.
Remove from oven and add topping.

Topping:

3 tbsp.	butter, melted	45 mL
4 tbsp.	brown sugar	60 mL
3 tbsp.	heavy cream	45 mL
3/4 cup	coconut	175 mL

Combine ingredients in saucepan and stir over low heat until warm.
Pour over cake.
Return to oven and put under broiler until topping bubbles and slightly browns.

BLUEBERRY ORANGE CAKE

3/4 cup	butter	175 mL
1 1/2 cups	white sugar	375 mL
3	eggs	3
1 tsp.	vanilla	5 mL
	finely chopped peel of 2 oranges	
2 cups	all-purpose flour	500 mL
3/4 cup	milk	175 mL
1/2 tsp.	baking powder	2 mL
2 cups	blueberries, lightly dusted with flour	500 mL

Preheat oven to 350°F (180°C).

Cream butter and gradually add sugar and vanilla.

Combine dry ingredients and add to butter mixture alternating with milk.

Fold in orange peel and blueberries. Do not over mix.

Bake for 50 to 55 minutes in medium-sized rectangular pan or large tube pan.

Let set 10 minutes before removing from pan.

Glaze while hot with topping OR frost with cream cheese icing when cold.

Topping:

3 tbsp.	orange juice concentrate	45 mL
1 cup	icing sugar, sifted	250 mL

Mix together well.

. . . Continued next page

BLUEBERRY ORANGE CAKE

Continued . . .

Cream Cheese Icing:

4 oz.	**cream cheese, softened**	125 g
1/4 cup	**butter, softened**	50 mL
2 cups	**icing sugar, sifted**	500 mL
1 tsp.	**vanilla**	5 mL

Cream cheese and butter.
Gradually add icing sugar and vanilla.
Beat well. If too thick, thin with milk.

CAROLINE'S BLUEBERRY CAKE

1 cup	white sugar	250 mL
1 1/2 cups	all-purpose flour	375 mL
2 tsp.	baking powder	2 mL
1/2 tsp.	salt	500 mL
3 tbsp.	butter, melted	45 mL
1	egg, add milk to make	1 cup (250 mL)
1 tsp.	vanilla	5 mL
2 cups	blueberries	500 mL

Preheat oven to 350°F (180°C).
Sift together dry ingredients.
Combine wet ingredients and blend well.
Add wet ingredients to dry and stir until well mixed.
Add blueberries.
Bake in square cake pan for 30 minutes.

BLUEBERRY COFFEECAKE

4	eggs, separated	4
1 3/4 cups	white sugar	425 mL
2 1/2 cups	all-purpose flour	625 mL
2 tsp.	baking powder	10 mL
1 tbsp.	vanilla	15 mL
1 cup	oil	250 mL
2	lemons, juice and grated rind	2
2 cups	blueberries, floured	500 mL

Preheat oven to 350°F (180°C).

Beat egg whites until foamy.

Add sugar, egg yolks, oil, vanilla, lemon juice and lemon rind.

Fold in dry ingredients and berries, reserving a few berries for bottom of pan.

Pour into 8 cup (2 L) dish and bake for 1 hour.

Nova Scotia produces over half of the total Canadian wild blueberry crop.

BRENDA'S BLUEBERRY BUCKLE

1/4 cup	butter, softened	50 mL
1/2 cup	white sugar	125 mL
1	egg	1
1/4 tsp.	lemon rind, grated	1 mL
4 tsp.	lemon juice	20 mL
1 cup	all-purpose flour	250 mL
1 tsp.	baking powder	5 mL
1/4 tsp.	salt	1 mL
1/4 cup	milk	50 mL
2 cups	blueberries	500 mL

Topping:

1/2 cup	white sugar	125 mL
1/4 cup	butter	50 mL
1/3 cup	all-purpose flour	75 mL
1/4 tsp.	lemon rind, grated	1 mL
dash	cinnamon	dash

Preheat oven to 350°F (180°C).
Cream butter and sugar.
Beat in egg, lemon rind and juice.
Mix dry ingredients together.
Blend into creamed mixture and add milk.
Put batter into greased pan and sprinkle blueberries, then topping, over mixture.
Bake for 45 minutes.

P.E.I. BLUEBERRY PUDDING

1/4 cup	shortening	60 mL
1 cup	all-purpose flour	250 mL
1/2 tsp.	salt	2 mL
1/2 cup	milk	125 mL
1/2 cup	white sugar	125 mL
1 tsp.	baking powder	5 mL
1	egg	1
1 tsp.	lemon flavouring	5 mL
1 1/2 to 2 cups	blueberries	375 to 500 mL
1/2 cup	white sugar	125 mL

Preheat oven to 375°F (190°C).

Cream shortening, 1/2 cup (125 mL) sugar and egg. Beat well.

Add milk.

Sift flour with baking powder and salt and add to creamed mixture.

Add flavouring.

Cover bottom of ovenproof dish with blueberries. Add sugar to sweeten.

Pour batter over fruit.

Bake for approximately 1 hour.

Serve warm with table cream or whipped cream.

ROBIN'S BLUEBERRY KUCHEN

1 cup plus 2 tbsp.	all-purpose flour, divided	250 mL plus 30 mL
pinch	salt	pinch
2 tbsp. plus 2/3 cup	white sugar, divided	30 mL plus 150 mL
1/2 cup	butter, softened	125 mL
1 tbsp.	vinegar	15 mL
5 cups	blueberries, divided	1.25 L
pinch	cinnamon	pinch

Preheat oven to 400°F (200°C).

Mix 1 cup (250 mL) flour, salt and 2 tbsp. (30 mL) sugar.

Cut in butter until mixture crumbles.

Sprinkle with vinegar.

Shape into a dough ball and press evenly over bottom and sides of a spring-form pan.

Pour in 3 cups (750 mL) berries.

Mix remaining flour with sugar and cinnamon.

Sprinkle over berries.

Bake on low rack in oven for 1 hour.

Remove from oven and sprinkle remaining berries over dessert.

Cool.

Remove rim of pan.

BLUEBERRY STREUDEL

3 or 4 sheets   **phyllo pastry**   **3 or 4 sheets**
                  butter, melted
                  1 recipe blueberry sauce (see page 63)

Preheat oven to 400°F (200°C).
Brush melted butter between pastry layers.
Spoon blueberry sauce onto phyllo layer, wrap tops of sheet over, tuck in, and roll up.
Bake on cookie sheet 20 minutes, or until puffy and crisp.
Sprinkle a sugar/cinnamon mixture on top of each roll.

BLUEBERRY PUDDING

1/4 cup	shortening	50 mL
3/4 cup	white sugar	175 mL
1	egg	1
2 1/4 cups	all-purpose flour	550 mL
2 tsp.	baking powder	10 mL
1/2 tsp.	salt	2 mL
1/2 cup	milk	125 mL
1 cup	blueberries	250 mL

Preheat oven to 350°F (180°C).
Cream together shortening, sugar and egg.
Stir together flour, baking powder and salt.
Blend dry ingredients into shortening mixture, alternately with milk.
Beat.
Stir in blueberries.
Pour into greased, shallow pan and bake for 40-45 minutes.
Cut into squares and serve with lemon sauce (see page 48).

LEMON SAUCE

1/2 cup	white sugar	125 mL
1 tbsp.	cornstarch	15 mL
pinch	salt	pinch
1 cup	boiling water	250 mL
2 tbsp.	butter	30 mL
2 tbsp.	lemon juice	30 mL
1	egg yolk, beaten	1

Mix sugar, cornstarch and salt in saucepan.
Add boiling water and stir over low heat until mixture thickens.
Remove from heat and stir in butter, lemon juice and egg yolk.

BLUEBERRY SHORTCAKE

2 cups	all-purpose flour	500 mL
1 tbsp.	baking powder	15 mL
1/2 tsp.	salt	2 mL
4 tbsp.	white sugar	60 mL
1/2 cup	shortening	125 mL
2/3 cup	milk	150 mL

Preheat oven to 425°F (220°C).

Combine dry ingredients, cut in shortening, add milk.

Pour into cake pan and bake for 7 minutes.

Cool.

Divide into small serving pieces.

Spoon blueberry sauce (see page 63) over cake, cover with another piece of cake, top with whipped cream and pour more sauce over all.

CAROLE'S BLUEBERRY DELIGHT

Step one:

1/2 cup	**butter, melted**	**125 mL**
2 cups	**graham wafers, crushed**	**500 mL**
2 tbsp.	**white sugar**	**30 mL**

Melt butter, mix in other ingredients.
Press mixture into bottom of 9'' by 13'' (approximately 20 by 30 cm) pan.

Step two:

8 oz.	**cream cheese, softened**	**250 g**
1/2 cup	**white sugar**	**125 mL**
2	**eggs**	**2**
	vanilla to taste	

Preheat oven to 350°F (180°C).
Mix ingredients together and spread over wafer mixture.
Bake for 15 to 20 minutes.

Step three:

4 cups	**blueberries**	**1 L**
3/4 cup	**white sugar**	**175 mL**
2 1/2 tbsp.	**cornstarch**	**35 to 40 mL**
	lemon juice, if desired	

Bring sugar and blueberries to a boil.
Mix cornstarch in water and add to boiling blueberries.
Add lemon juice, if desired.
Spread over cooled cream cheese and wafer layers.
Top with whipped cream.

SAUCY BLUEBERRY ROLL

2 cups	all-purpose flour	500 mL
1/2 tsp.	salt	2 mL
4 tsp.	baking powder	20 mL
2 tbsp.	white sugar	30 mL
4 tbsp.	oil	60 mL
1/2 cup	milk	125 mL
2/3 cup	blueberries	150 mL
1 tbsp.	sugar	15 mL
2 tsp.	all-purpose flour	10 mL
	butter	

Preheat oven to 400°F (200°C).
Sift together flour, salt, baking powder and sugar.
Add oil mixed with milk.
Roll mixture into a rectangle about 1/4" (.5 cm) thick.
Sprinkle berries with sugar and flour. Spoon on top of dough.
Dot with butter.
Roll up like a jelly roll.
Cut into pieces about 1" (2cm approximately) and place in baking pan.
Brush with milk.
Bake for 30 minutes.

Serve with brown sugar sauce (see page 36) or lemon sauce (see page 48).

Cookies~Squares

BLUEBERRY COOKIES

1/2 cup	butter, softened	125 mL
1/2 cup	white sugar	125 mL
1/2 cup	brown sugar	125 mL
2	eggs, beaten	2
1 1/2 cups	all-purpose flour	375 mL
1 tsp.	baking powder	5 mL
1 tsp.	baking soda	5 mL
1/2 tsp.	salt	2 mL
1/3 cup	sour milk	75 mL
1 tsp.	lemon rind, grated	5 mL
1 cup	blueberries	250 mL

Preheat oven to 350°F (180°C).
Cream butter and sugars.
Add eggs and beat.
Stir in dry ingredients, alternately with the sour milk.
Fold in blueberries and lemon rind.
Drop by spoonful onto greased cookie sheets.
Bake for 12-15 minutes.

MICROWAVE BROWNIE SURPRISE

2	eggs	2
1 cup	white sugar	250 mL
1/2 tsp.	salt	2 mL
1 tsp.	vanilla	5 mL
1/2 cup	butter, melted	125 mL
3/4 cup	all-purpose flour	175 mL
1/2 cup	cocoa	125 mL
1/2 cup	pecans, chopped	125 mL
1/2 cup	blueberries	125 mL
2 tbsp.	icing sugar	30 mL

To melt butter, heat for 30 seconds on High.

In a small bowl mix eggs, sugar, salt and vanilla at medium speed for about 1 minute or until light and fluffy.

Add melted butter and continue to blend.

Mix in flour and cocoa at low speed.

Stir in pecans.

In a greased, square glass ovenproof dish, spread a thin layer of batter.

Sprinkle blueberries over top and cover with remaining batter.

Microwave on High for approximately 6 minutes, rotating dish after each 2 minutes.

Cool for a few minutes, then cut into squares.

Remove from pan and roll each square in icing sugar to dust.

OATMEAL BLUEBERRY SQUARES

1 1/2 cups	oatmeal	375 mL
1 cup	all-purpose flour	250 mL
1 cup	brown sugar	250 mL
pinch	salt	pinch
1 1/2 tsp.	baking powder	7 mL
1 cup	butter, melted	250 mL
2 cups	blueberries	500 mL
2 tbsp.	cornstarch	30 mL
1/2 cup	white sugar	125 mL
1 tbsp.	lemon juice	5 mL
1/4 cup	water	50 mL

Preheat oven to 350°F (180°C).

Combine first six ingredients.

Spread half of the mixture in a square cake pan.

Save the remainder for topping.

Prepare filling: Combine blueberries, cornstarch, white sugar, lemon juice and water in a saucepan.

Cook over medium heat until thickened.

Cool to warm temperature and spread over oatmeal mixture.

Top with reserved oatmeal mixture.

Bake until golden.

BLUEBERRY SQUARES

3 tbsp.	butter, softened	45 mL
1/3 cup	white sugar	75 mL
2	egg yolks	2
2/3 cup	all-purpose flour	150 mL
1 tsp.	baking powder	5 mL
1/4 tsp.	salt	1 mL
1/4 cup	milk	50 mL
1/4 tsp.	vanilla	1 mL

Preheat oven to 350°F (180°C).
Cream butter and sugar. Beat in egg yolks.
Add dry ingredients alternately with blended liquids.
Turn mixture into greased 8" x 8" (20 cm x 20 cm) pan.
Bake for 20 minutes.

Topping:

2	egg whites	2
1/4 tsp.	salt	1 mL
6 tbsp.	white sugar	90 mL
1 cup	blueberries	250 mL

Beat egg whites, gradually adding sugar and salt.
Fold in blueberries and spread over baked mixture.
Bake at 300°F (150°C) until topping is slightly browned.

KAY'S ALMOND BERRY DROPS

1 cup	butter, softened	250 mL
1/2 cup	white sugar	125 mL
1/2 cup	brown sugar	125 mL
1	egg	1
1 tsp.	baking soda	5 mL
2 tsp.	cream of tartar	10 mL
1 tsp.	almond flavouring	5 mL
1/2 tsp.	salt	2 mL
2 cups	all-purpose flour	500 mL
1/2 cup	blueberries	125 mL

Preheat oven to 350°F (180°C).
Cream butter and add sugar gradually.
Beat egg slightly and stir into butter mixture.
Combine all dry ingredients, and gradually add to butter mixture.
Add almond flavouring.
Roll mixture into little balls and place onto greased cookie sheet.
Firm down with a fork and press a few berries into each cookie.
Bake for 10 minutes.

Etcetera

BLUEBERRY SAUCE

2/3 cup	white sugar	150 mL
2 tbsp.	cornstarch	30 mL
1/4 cup	water	50 mL
1 tbsp.	lemon juice	15 mL
pinch	salt	pinch
4 cups	blueberries	1 L

Combine sugar and cornstarch, add water, lemon juice and salt, cook over medium heat until thickened.
Add blueberries and cook until sauce is clear.
Chill, covered tightly.
Keeps for 3 or 4 days if stored in refrigerator.
Serve with ice cream, pudding, pancakes.

Makes 3 cups (750 mL).

Learn more about the wonderful world of the wild blueberry — visit the Blueberry Patch at the Nova Scotia-New Brunswick border!

CHILLED BLUEBERRY SOUP

2 tbsp.	**potato flour**	30 mL
3 cups	**water**	750 mL
4 cups	**blueberries**	1 L
3/4 cup	**sugar**	175 mL

Mix the potato flour in a little cold water and set aside.
In a pot, combine water, sugar and blueberries and bring to a boil.
Stir in the potato 'paste' and bring again to a boil.
Cool and cover.
Top with a dollop of whipped cream before serving.

Serves four.

BLUEBERRY JAM

2 cups	**blueberries**	500 mL
1/2 cup	**liquid honey**	125 mL
	grated rind of one small lemon	

Combine all ingredients in a 3 quart (3L) pot and bring to a boil.
Simmer, uncovered, over low heat for 40 to 45 minutes.
Stir frequently, especially during final cooking stages.
Remove from heat when jam is thick.
Store in clean jar in refrigerator.

SUSAN'S BLUEBERRY QUEEN JAM

2 cups	**red raspberries**	500 mL
2 cups	**blueberries**	500 mL
6 1/2 cups	**white sugar**	1.5 L plus 125 mL
1/3 cup	**lemon juice**	75 mL
1/3 cup	**liquid fruit pectin**	75 mL

Crush berries and add lemon juice.

Stir in sugar, place over high heat and bring ingredients to a rolling boil and boil rapidly for 1 minute, stirring constantly.

Remove from heat and stir in pectin.

Skim off any foam with a metal spoon.

Stir and skim for 5 minutes more to cool slightly and prevent floating fruit.

Ladle immediately into sterile jars and cover with hot paraffin.

Makes 6 to 7 cups of jam, depending on juice of berries. (Prepare 3 (½L) jars and one smaller size).

If using sweetened, frozen raspberries, decrease sugar to 5 ½ cups.

SPARKLING SALAD

1 package	lemon gelatin	1 package
2 tbsp.	vinegar	30 mL
1/2 cup	grated carrots OR finely chopped celery	125 mL
1/2 cup	blueberries	125 mL

Prepare gelatin according to package directions.
Add vinegar.
Pour into individual moulds or one large bowl/mould.
Cool in refrigerator just until it begins to set.
Stir in carrots (or celery) and berries.
Refrigerate until firm.

Serves four to six.

SPICED BLUEBERRY SALAD

2 cups	blueberries	500 mL
2/3 tsp.	allspice	3 mL
1 stick	cinnamon	1 stick
pinch	salt	pinch
2/3 tsp.	whole cloves	3 mL
1 tbsp.	gelatin	15 mL
1/3 cup	water	75 mL
1 tbsp.	vinegar	15 mL
3 tbsp.	lemon juice	45 mL

Soften gelatin in water.

In a saucepan, combine first five ingredients and simmer until blueberries soften slightly.

Stir and remove from heat.

Let cool for a few minutes and stir in the gelatin.

Add vinegar and lemon juice.

Pour into individual moulds or one large mould.

Unmould and serve on lettuce.

Serves four.

ACORN SQUASH WITH BLUEBERRIES

2	acorn squash	2
1/4 cup	brown sugar	50 mL
3/4 tsp.	cinnamon	4 mL
1 tsp.	cornstarch	5 mL
1/4 tsp.	salt	1 mL
1 cup	blueberries	250 mL
3/4 cup	diced apple	175 mL
1 tbsp.	butter	15 mL
pinch	salt	pinch

For microwave:

Cut squash in half and remove seeds.

Place squash cut side up on a flat plate.

Cover with plastic wrap and microwave on high for 10 minutes, rotating after 5 minutes. Remove from oven and keep warm.

Fold back wrap carefully after squash is cooked.

In a small bowl, combine all ingredients except butter.

Microwave on high for 4 minutes.

Stir in butter and pour into each squash cavity.

For conventional oven:

Preheat oven to 350°F (180°C).

Cut squash in half and remove seeds.

Place squash cut side up in an ovenproof baking dish filled with enough water to just cover bottom of pan.

In a small bowl, combine the remaining ingredients except butter.

Spoon mixture into each squash cavity. Dot with butter.

Cover and bake for 45 minutes.

Serves four.

RHODA'S CANDY

2 cups	semi-sweet or sweet chocolate	500 mL
1/4 cup	butter	50 mL
or less		or less
2 cups	blueberries	500 mL

Combine chocolate and butter in a bowl over hot water.

Stir until melted.

Remove from heat and drop a teaspoon in the bottom of a chocolate mould.

Turn mould so chocolate coats sides.

Place a few berries in each form, cover each with 2 teaspoons of chocolate.

Chill.

Preparation time: 20 to 30 minutes.

An easy glaze is made simply by melting red currant or apple jelly. As it melts, add a few drops of water until of spreading consistency.

BLUEBERRY POPS

1 envelope **blueberry drink mix**
water (amount according to
package instructions)

Mix contents of package.
Pour into popsicle trays.
Freeze until firm.

BLUENOSE

2 cups	**clear blueberry juice, cold**	**500 mL**
1/2 cup	**rum**	**125 mL**
	lemon wedge	
	mint sprigs	

Rub lemon wedge around edge of glasses before placing in freezer to frost.
Combine blueberry juice with rum.
Serve over crushed ice in frosted glasses.
Garnish with mint sprigs.

Serves four.

BLUEBERRY TEA

	hot tea	
1/2 oz.	**Grand Marnier**	15 mL
1/2 oz.	**Amaretto**	15 mL

In a cup, place each of the liqueurs, then add tea.

Index

Muffins

Blueberry Buttermilk Muffins	1
Blueberry Pumpkin Muffins	2
Blueberry Oatmeal Muffins	3
Sharon's Blueberry Muffins	4
Blueberry Bran Muffins	5
Microwave Blueberry Muffins	6
Jiffy Blueberry Muffins	7
Blueberry Maple Muffins With Streusel Topping	8
Anna's Blueberry Muffins	9

Breads - Biscuits

Blueberry Biscuits	13
Blueberry Scotch Scones	14
Marjorie's Blueberry Orange Bread	15
Blueberry Gingerbread	16
Joyce's Blueberry Tea Loaves	17
Anne's Orange Blue Loaf	19
Lemon Blueberry Loaf	20

Desserts

Hope's No Bake Blueberry Pie	23
Blueberry Pie	24
Stonehouse Blueberry Pie	25
Orange'N Berry Sponge Pie	26
Mac's Favourite Blueberry Cream Pie	27
Jean's Pound Cake	28
Blueberry Sauce (for trifle)	29
Gram's Cornstarch Pudding	30
Walker's Special Trifle	31
Mark's Cheesecake	32
Promotion Cheesecake	33
Lina's Cupcake Cheese Cakes	34
Blueberry Dessert	35
Brown Sugar Sauce	36
Exhibition Favourite Yogurt Cake	37
Gwen's Hurry-Up Cake	38

Blueberry Orange Cake 39
Caroline's Blueberry Cake 41
Blueberry Coffeecake 42
Brenda's Blueberry Buckle 43
P.E.I. Blueberry Pudding 44
Robin's Blueberry Kuchen 45
Blueberry Streudel 46
Blueberry Pudding 47
Lemon Sauce 48
Blueberry Shortcake 49
Carole's Blueberry Delight 50
Saucy Blueberry Roll 51

Cookies - Squares
Blueberry Cookies 55
Microwave Brownie Surprise 56
Oatmeal Blueberry Squares 57
Blueberry Squares 58
Kay's Almond Berry Drops 59

Etcetera
Blueberry Sauce 63
Chilled Blueberry Soup 64
Blueberry Jam 65
Susan's Blueberry Queen Jam 66
Sparkling Salad 67
Spiced Blueberry Salad 68
Acorn Squash With Blueberries 69
Rhoda's Candy 70
Blueberry Pops 71
Bluenose 72
Blueberry Tea 73